word mas[ter]

Quotations

"ALL ANIMALS ARE EQUAL. BUT SOME ANIMALS ARE MORE EQUAL THAN OTHERS."

Kingfisher Books

Kingfisher Books, Grisewood & Dempsey Ltd,
Elsley House, 24-30 Great Titchfield Street, London
W1P 7AD

First published in 1992 by Kingfisher Books
10 9 8 7 6 5 4 3 2 1

The material in this edition was previously published by Kingfisher Books in the *Kingfisher Book of Words* 1991

© Grisewood & Dempsey Ltd 1991, 1992

All rights reserved. No part of this publication may be reproduced, stored in a retrieval system or transmitted by any means, electronic, mechanical, photocopying or otherwise, without the prior permission of the publisher.

British Library Cataloguing in Publication Data
A catalogue record for this book is available from the British Library.

ISBN 0 86272 903 3

General Editor: John Grisewood
Edited by Nicola Barber
Illustrations by Peter Stevenson (Kathy Jakeman Illustration)
Designed by Robert Wheeler
Cover design by Terry Woodley
Phototypeset by Southern Positives and Negatives (SPAN), Lingfield, Surrey
Printed in Spain

MODERN QUOTATIONS

Everyone uses quotations in their everyday speech, sometimes without realizing that they are, in fact, quoting the words of someone else. Probably the most-quoted of all people is William Shakespeare. There exist several large volumes which are entirely devoted to quotations from his works. This book concentrates on modern quotations, mostly first used in the present century. A key-word system is used to find a particular quotation – for example, if you want to look up who wrote 'O to be in England, now that April's there', you look up **England** and find that the quotation was originated by Robert Browning. If you want to know more about the person quoted you can turn to the alphabetical list at the end of the book. The quotations in boxes are, in fact, misquotations.

A

abnormal
If it weren't for the fact that all of us are slightly abnormal, there wouldn't be any point in giving each person a separate name.
UGO BETTI.

abstract
Abstract art? A product of the untalented, sold by the unprincipled to the utterly bewildered.
AL CAPP.

acting
Acting is not a profession for adults.
LAURENCE OLIVIER.
The general consensus seems to be that I don't act at all.
GARY COOPER.
The hardest kind of acting works only if you look as if you are not acting at all.
HENRY FONDA.

actors
Seventy-five per cent of being successful as an actor is pure luck. The rest is just endurance.
GENE HACKMAN.
Actors and burglars work better at night.
SIR CEDRIC HARDWICKE.

adapting
Human creatures have a marvellous power of adapting themselves to necessity.
GEORGE GISSING.

adults
Adults are obsolete children.
DR SEUSS.

adventure
Adventure is the result of poor planning.
COL. BLASHFORD-SNELL.

advice
No-one wants advice – only corroboration.
JOHN STEINBECK.

alive
It's a funny old world; a man's lucky if he gets out alive.
W.C. FIELDS.

> **alone** I want to be alone. GRETA GARBO. Her true words were: "I like to be alone.".

MODERN QUOTATIONS

America
America is God's Crucible, the Great Melting-Pot.
　　　　　　　　ISRAEL ZANGWILL.

amused
We are not amused.
　　　　　　　　QUEEN VICTORIA.

angels
Angels can fly because they take themselves lightly.
　　　　　　　　G.K. CHESTERTON.

antique
An antique is something that's been useless so long it's still in good condition.
　　　　　　　　FRANKLIN P. JONES.

applaud
If they liked you, they didn't applaud – they just let you live.
　　　　　　　　BOB HOPE.

archaeologist
An archaeologist is the best husband a woman can have; the older she gets the more interested he is in her.
　　　　　　　　AGATHA CHRISTIE.

arguing
I am not arguing with you – I am telling you.
　　　　　　　　JAMES MCNEILL WHISTLER.

argument
The best way I know to win an argument is to start by being in the right.
　　　　　　　　LORD HAILSHAM.
The only way to get the best of an argument is to avoid it.
　　　　　　　　DALE CARNEGIE.

armour
Armour is the kind of clothing worn by a man whose tailor was a blacksmith.
　　　　　　　　AMBROSE BIERCE.

assassination
Assassination is the extreme form of censorship.
　　　　　　　　GEORGE BERNARD SHAW.

atheist
I am an atheist still, thank God.
　　　　　　　　LUIS BUÑUEL.
The worst moment for an atheist is when he feels grateful and doesn't know who to thank.
　　　　　　　　WENDY WARD.

audience
If all the world's a stage, and all the men and women merely players, where do all the audiences come from?
　　　　　　　　DENIS NORDEN.
A work of art does not exist without its audience.
　　　　　　　　RICHARD HAMILTON.
The only real teacher of acting is the audience.
　　　　　　　　GEORGE C. SCOTT.

average
Most people are such fools that it really is no compliment to say that a man is above average.
　　　　　　　　W. SOMERSET MAUGHAM.

MODERN QUOTATIONS

B

badly
If a thing is worth doing it is worth doing badly.
G.K. CHESTERTON.

ball
The ball is man's most disastrous invention, not excluding the wheel.
ROBERT MORLEY.

bank
Banks lend you money as people lend you an umbrella when the sun is shining and want it back when it starts to rain.
SIR EDWARD BEDDINGTON-BEHRENS.
A bank is a place that will lend you money if you can prove that you don't need it.
BOB HOPE.

bat
Twinkle, twinkle little bat!
How I wonder what you're at!
LEWIS CARROLL.

beard
An irregular greying beard was a decoration to a face which badly needed assistance.
EDGAR WALLACE.
I grew a beard for Nero, in *Quo Vadis*, but Metro-Goldwyn-Mayer thought it didn't look real, so I had to wear a false one.
PETER USTINOV.

beautiful
Remember that the most beautiful things in the world are the most useless; peacocks and lilies for instance.
JOHN RUSKIN.

THE BIGGER THEY COME THE HARDER THEY FALL.

Bible
The number one book of the ages was written by a committee, and it was called the Bible.
LOUIS B. MAYER.

bigger
The bigger they come, the harder they fall.
ROBERT FITZSIMMONS.

billiards
Proficiency at billiards is proof of a misspent youth.
HERBERT SPENCER.

blind
In the country of the blind the one-eyed man is king.
H.G. WELLS.

5

MODERN QUOTATIONS

Did you know that Ambrose Bierce said that a bore is a fellow who talks when you want him to listen.

blushing
Man is the only animal that blushes – or needs to.
MARK TWAIN.

boaster
A boaster is not always a liar.
ERIC PARTRIDGE.

books
The only books I have in my library are books that other people have lent me.
ANATOLE FRANCE.

When I am dead, I hope it may be said: "His sins were scarlet, but his books were read."
HILAIRE BELLOC.

bore
A fellow who talks when you wish him to listen.
AMBROSE BIERCE.

box
We give people a box in the suburbs. It's called a house, and every night they sit in it staring at another box, in the morning they run off to another box called an office, and at the weekends they get into another box, on wheels this time, and grope their way through endless traffic jams.
CAROLINE KELLY.

boxing
Boxing is glamorized violence.
LORD TAYLOR OF GRYFE.

bravery
There is no such thing as bravery; only degrees of fear.
JOHN WAINWRIGHT.

breakfast
If you want to eat well in England, eat three breakfasts.
W. SOMERSET MAUGHAM.

brother
I want to be the white man's brother, not his brother-in-law.
MARTIN LUTHER KING.

buck
The buck stops here.
HARRY S. TRUMAN (*Sign on President Truman's desk*)

C

cards
When a man tells me he's going to put all his cards on the table, I always look up his sleeve.
LORD HORE-BELISHA.

care
If I'd known how old I was going to be I'd have taken better care of myself.
ADOLPH ZUKOR.

celebrity
A celebrity is a person who works hard all his life to become known, then wears dark glasses to avoid being recognized.
FRED ALLEN.

MODERN QUOTATIONS

cheese
How can you govern a country which produces 246 different kinds of cheese?
CHARLES DE GAULLE.

child
When a child is grown up, it's time the parents learned to stand on their own feet.
FRANCIS HOPE.

cinema
The cinema is not a slice of life. It's a piece of cake.
ALFRED HITCHCOCK.
Cinema is the most beautiful fraud in the world.
JEAN-LUC GODARD.

city
The city is not a concrete jungle, it is a human zoo.
DESMOND MORRIS.

civil servants
Some civil servants are neither servants nor civil.
WINSTON CHURCHILL.

clever
I know I'm not clever, but I'm always right.
J.M. BARRIE.

club
I don't want to belong to any club that will accept me as a member.
GROUCHO MARX.

comeback
I'm always making a comeback, but nobody ever tells me where I've been.
BILLIE HOLLIDAY.

comedian
A comedian does funny things; a good comedian does things funny.
BUSTER KEATON.

comedy
Comedy is simply a funny way of being serious.
PETER USTINOV.
All I need to make a comedy is a park, a policeman and a pretty girl.
CHARLIE CHAPLIN.

comment
Comment is free, but facts are sacred.
C.P. SCOTT.

common man
The century on which we are entering – the century which will come out of this war – can be and must be the century of the common man.
HENRY WALLACE.

composers
Composers should write tunes that chauffeurs and errand boys can whistle.
SIR THOMAS BEECHAM.

I DON'T WANT TO BELONG TO ANY CLUB THAT WILL ACCEPT ME AS A MEMBER

7

MODERN QUOTATIONS

computer
To err is human, but to really foul things up requires a computer.
PAUL EHRLICH.

conscience
I cannot and I will not cut my conscience to fit this year's fashions.
LILLIAN HELLMAN.

consequences
You can do anything in this world if you are prepared to take the consequences.
W. SOMERSET MAUGHAM.

contract
A verbal contract isn't worth the paper it's written on.
SAM GOLDWYN.

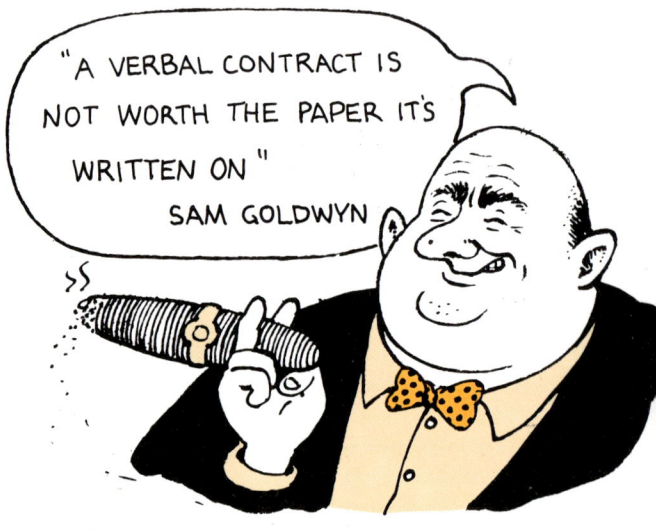

cook
The cook was a good cook, as cooks go; and as cooks go, she went.
'SAKI' (H.H. MUNRO).

courtesy
Courtesy is not dead. It has merely taken refuge in Great Britain.
GEORGES DUHAMEL.

cricket
There is one great similarity between music and cricket. There are slow movements in both.
NEVILLE CARDUS.

customer
The customer is always right.
H. GORDON SELFRIDGE.

cynic
A cynic is a man who knows the price of everything and the value of nothing.
OSCAR WILDE.

D

day
It was such a lovely day I thought it was a pity to get up.
W. SOMERSET MAUGHAM.

MODERN QUOTATIONS

dead
What I like about Clive
Is that he is no longer alive.
There is a great deal to be said
For being dead.
> E.C. BENTLEY.

death
I'm not afraid to die; I just don't want to be there when it happens.
> WOODY ALLEN.

After the first death, there is no other.
> DYLAN THOMAS.

I have lost friends, some by death, others through sheer inability to cross the street.
> VIRGINIA WOOLF.

devil
It is stupid of modern civilization to have given up believing in the devil when he is the only explanation of it.
> RONALD KNOX.

diary
Keep a diary and one day it will keep you.
> MAE WEST.

die
To die will be an awfully big adventure.
> J.M. BARRIE.

Die, my dear doctor? That's the last thing I shall do.
> LORD PALMERSTON.

directions
Lord Ronald ... flung himself upon his horse and rode madly off in all directions.
> STEPHEN LEACOCK.

---

discretion Discretion is the better part of valour. WILLIAM SHAKESPEARE. The correct quotation is: 'The better part of valour is discretion.'.

---

disgruntled
I could see that, if not actually disgruntled, he was far from being gruntled.
> P.G. WODEHOUSE.

dog
A dog is the only thing on earth that loves you more than you love yourself.
> JOSH BILLINGS.

Any man who hates dogs and babies can't be all bad.
> LEO C. ROSTEN.

The noblest of all dogs is the hot dog; it feeds the hand that bites it.
> LAURENCE J. PETER.

dontopedalogy
Dontopedalogy is the science of opening your mouth and putting your foot in it.
> PRINCE PHILIP (DUKE OF EDINBURGH.)

down and out
When you are down and out something always turns up – and it is usually the noses of your friends.
> ORSON WELLES.

MODERN QUOTATIONS

dreams
But I, being poor, have only my dreams;
I have spread my dreams under your feet;
Tread softly because you tread on my dreams.
                          W.B. YEATS.

drowning
I was much too far out all my life,
And not waving but drowning.
                        STEVIE SMITH.

dull
There are no dull subjects. There are only dull writers.
                        H.L. MENCKEN.

dying
Dying is a very dull, dreary affair. My advice to you is to have nothing whatever to do with it.
          W. SOMERSET MAUGHAM.

Dying
Is an art, like everything else.
I do it exceptionally well.
                      SYLVIA PLATH.

"ALL ANIMALS ARE EQUAL. BUT SOME ANIMALS ARE MORE EQUAL THAN OTHERS."

E

ears
His ears make him look like a taxi with both doors open.
      HOWARD HUGHES (referring to Clark Gable).

It's all very well to be able to write books, but can you waggle your ears?
                      J.M. BARRIE.

earth
The meek shall inherit the earth, but not its mineral rights.
                      J. PAUL GETTY.

earthquake
What we want is a story that starts with an earthquake and works its way up to a climax.
                    SAM GOLDWYN.

east
Oh, East is East, and West is West, and never the twain shall meet.
                  RUDYARD KIPLING.

education
Education has for its object the formation of character.
                  HERBERT SPENCER.

Education is what survives when what has been learned has been forgotten.
                  B.F. SKINNER.

MODERN QUOTATIONS

elephant
I have a memory like an elephant. In fact, elephants often consult me.
NOËL COWARD.

enemies
Do not fear when your enemies criticize you. Beware when they applaud.
VO DONG GIANG.

England
That there's some corner of a foreign field
That is for ever England.
RUPERT BROOKE.

Oh, to be in England
Now that April's there.
ROBERT BROWNING.

English
This is the sort of English up with which I will not put.
WINSTON CHURCHILL.

An Englishman, even if he is alone, forms an orderly queue of one.
GEORGE MIKES.

An Englishman thinks he is moral only when he is uncomfortable.
GEORGE BERNARD SHAW.

enjoy
The only way to enjoy anything in this life is to earn it first.
GINGER ROGERS.

equal
All animals are equal, but some animals are more equal than others.
GEORGE ORWELL.

All men are born equal, but quite a few eventually get over it.
LORD MANCROFT.

evolution
Evolution is far more important than living.
ERNST JUNGER.

excuses
Several excuses are always less convincing than one.
ALDOUS HUXLEY.

F

facts
The trouble with facts is that there are so many of them.
SAMUEL MCCHORD CROTHERS.

Generally, the theories we believe we call facts and the facts we disbelieve we call theories.
FELIX COHEN.

failure
There is much to be said for failure. It is more interesting than success.
MAX BEERBOHM.

There is no formula for success. But there is a formula for failure, and that is trying to please everybody.
NICHOLAS RAY.

fairies
There are fairies at the bottom of our garden!
ROSE FYLEMAN.

famous
It took me fifteen years to discover I had no talent for writing, but I couldn't give it up, because by that time I was too famous.
ROBERT BENCHLEY.

The tragedy of being famous is that you have to devote so much time to being famous.
PABLO PICASSO.

fancy
A little of what you fancy does you good.
MARIE LLOYD.

MODERN QUOTATIONS

IMPRISONED IN EVERY FAT MAN A THIN ONE IS WILDLY SIGNALING TO BE LET OUT

LET ME OUT!

fat
Imprisoned in every fat man a thin one is wildly signalling to be let out.
　　　　　　　　　　CYRIL CONNOLLY.

fate
I am the master of my fate;
I am the captain of my soul.
　　　　　　　　　　W.E. HENLEY.

Fate keeps on happening.
　　　　　　　　　　ANITA LOOS.

father
And when did you last see your father?
　　　　　　　　　　W.F. YEAMES.

fear
The only thing we have to fear is fear itself.
　　　　　　　　　　FRANKLIN D. ROOSEVELT.

We fear something before we hate it. A child who fears noises becomes a man who hates noises.
　　　　　　　　　　CYRIL CONNOLLY.

Fear is essential. It is like a drug.
　　　　　　　　　　LUIS MIGUEL DOMINGUIN.

female
For the female of the species is more deadly than the male.
　　　　　　　　　　RUDYARD KIPLING.

fence
If the fence is strong enough I'll sit on it.
　　　　　　　　　　CYRIL SMITH.

few
Never in the field of human conflict was so much owed by so many to so few.
　　　　　　　　　　WINSTON CHURCHILL (*1940*).

fight
We shall fight on the beaches, we shall fight on the landing grounds, we shall fight in the fields and in the streets, we shall fight in the hills; we shall never surrender.
　　　　　　　　　　WINSTON CHURCHILL (*1940*).

film
Every film should have a beginning, a middle and an end – but not necessarily in that order.
　　　　　　　　　　JEAN-LUC GODARD.

A film is never really good unless the camera is an eye in the head of a poet.
　　　　　　　　　　ORSON WELLES.

firm
I am firm. You are obstinate. He is a pig-headed fool.
　　　　　　　　　　KATHARINE WHITEHORN.

fisherman
All you need to be a fisherman is patience and a worm.
　　　　　　　　　　HERB SHRINER.

flowers
Where have all the flowers gone?
The young girls picked them every one.
　　　　　　　　　　PETE SEEGER.

MODERN QUOTATIONS

"I AM FIRM. YOU ARE OBSTINATE. HE IS A PIG-HEADED FOOL"

folk-singer
A folk-singer is someone who sings through his nose by ear.
        ANON.

food
On the Continent, people have good food; in England people have good table manners.
        GEORGE MIKES

football
Some people think football is a matter of life and death. . . . I can assure you it is much more serious than that.
        BILL SHANKLY.

friend
A friend in need is a friend to be avoided.
        LORD SAMUEL.

I do not believe that friends are necessarily the people you like best, they are merely the people who got there first.
        PETER USTINOV.

funny
What do you mean, funny? Funny peculiar or funny ha-ha?
        IAN HAY.

future
I have seen the future, and it works.
        LINCOLN STEFFENS.

I never think of the future. It comes soon enough.
        ALBERT EINSTEIN.

The best thing about the future is that it only comes one day at a time.
        DEAN ACHESON.

G

gamesmanship
Or the Art of Winning Games without Actually Cheating.
        STEPHEN POTTER.

genius
The genius of Einstein leads to Hiroshima.
        PABLO PICASSO.

Genius is one per cent inspiration and ninety-nine per cent perspiration.
        THOMAS A. EDISON.

"A FOLK SINGER IS SOMEONE WHO SINGS THROUGH HIS NOSE BY EAR."   *"FOL DE ROL FOL DE RAY"*

MODERN QUOTATIONS

gentleman
The English country gentleman galloping after a fox – the unspeakable in full pursuit of the uneatable.
OSCAR WILDE.

gluttony
"What I like about gluttony," a bishop I once knew used to say, "is that it doesn't hurt anyone else.".
MONICA FURLONG.

goal
You've got a goal. I've got a goal. Now all we need is a football team.
GROUCHO MARX.

golf
Golf is a game whose aim is to hit a very small ball into an even smaller hole, with weapons singularly ill-designed for the purpose.
WINSTON CHURCHILL.

good
On the whole human beings want to be good, but not too good, and not quite all the time.
GEORGE ORWELL.

goodness
Goodness is easier to recognize than to define.
W.H. AUDEN.

gourmet
A gourmet is just a glutton with brains.
PHILIP W. HABERMAN JR.

greatest
I am the greatest.
MUHAMMAD ALI.

grown-ups
One of the most obvious facts about grown-ups to a child is that they have forgotten what it is like to be a child.
RANDALL JARRELL.

guest
The art of being a good guest is to know when to leave.
PRINCE PHILIP (DUKE OF EDINBURGH).

guilty
It is better that ten guilty persons escape than one innocent suffer.
SIR WILLIAM BLACKSTONE.

MODERMN QUOTATIONS

H

haircut
Don't ask the barber whether you need a haircut.
> DANIEL S. GREENBERG.

happiness
One should never let one's happiness depend on other people.
> H. GRANVILLE BARKER.

Only in romantic novels are the beautiful guaranteed happiness.
> LADY CYNTHIA ASQUITH.

There is no such thing as the pursuit of happiness, but there is the discovery of joy.
> JOYCE GRENFELL.

happy
Even if we can't be happy, we must always be cheerful.
> IRVING KRISTOL.

hatchet
No one ever forgets where he buried the hatchet.
> KIM HUBBARD.

health
Too much health is unhealthy.
> LEO C. ROSTEN.

healthy
Early to rise and early to bed
Makes a male healthy, wealthy and dead.
> JAMES THURBER.

heaven
If you go to Heaven without being naturally qualified for it, you will not enjoy yourself there.
> GEORGE BERNARD SHAW.

hell
In hell there is no other punishment than to begin over and over again the tasks left unfinished in your lifetime.
> ANDRÉ GIDE.

heroes
People are only heroes when they cannot do anything else.
> PAUL CLAUDEL.

hesitates
He who hesitates is sometimes saved.
> JAMES THURBER.

historian
The novelist is the historian of the present. The historian is the novelist of the past.
> GEORGES DUHAMEL.

history
History, Stephen said, is a nightmare from which I am trying to awake.
> JAMES JOYCE.

History is an endless repetition of the wrong way of living.
> LAWRENCE DURRELL.

History teaches us that men and nations behave wisely once they have exhausted all other alternatives.
> ABBA EBAN.

The history of the world is the record of a man in quest of his daily bread and butter.
> H.W. VAN LOON.

Hitler
Hitler was a profoundly *uneducated* man of genius; there could be nothing more dangerous...
> A.L. ROWSE.

hole
A hole is nothing at all, but you can break your neck on it.
> AUSTIN O'MALLEY.

MODERN QUOTATIONS

holidays
Term, holidays, term, holidays, till we leave school, and then work, work, work till we die.
C.S. LEWIS.

Hollywood
Hollywood – a place where the inmates are in charge of the asylum.
LAURENCE STALLINGS.

home
Too many young people are beginning to regard home as a filling station by day and a parking place for the night.
REV. WILLIAM JOYCE.

hope
A poet's hope: to be, like some valley cheese, local, but prized elsewhere.
W.H. AUDEN.

horse
A horse is dangerous at both ends and uncomfortable in the middle.
IAN FLEMING.

host
The happy host makes a sad guest.
HAROLD ACTON.

house
A house is a machine for living in.
LE CORBUSIER.

human
A human being: an ingenious assembly of portable plumbing.
CHRISTOPHER MORLEY.

The human species is, to some extent, the result of mistakes which arrested our development and prevented us from assuming the somewhat unglamorous form of our primitive ancestors.
JONATHAN MILLER.

humour
Humour is practically the only thing about which the English are utterly serious.
MALCOLM MUGGERIDGE.

I have a fine sense of the ridiculous, but no sense of humour.
EDWARD ALBEE.

I

ill
One of the minor pleasures of life is to be slightly ill.
HAROLD NICOLSON.

influence
How to win friends and influence people.
DALE CARNEGIE.

AN INGENIOUS ASSEMBLY OF PORTABLE PLUMBING.

MODERN QUOTATIONS

J

K

jazz
What they call jazz is just the music of people's emotions.
　　　　　　　　WILLIE 'THE LION' SMITH.

joke
A joke isn't a joke until someone laughs.
　　　　　　　　MICHAEL CRAWFORD.

journalists
Journalists say a thing they know isn't true, in the hope that if they keep on saying it long enough it *will* be true.
　　　　　　　　ARNOLD BENNETT.

justice
Justice should not only be done, but should manifestly and undoubtedly be seen to be done.
　　　　　　　　LORD HEWART.

kids
There are three ways to get something done; do it yourself, hire someone, or forbid your kids to do it.
　　　　　　　　MONTA CRANE.

killed
Was it you or your brother who was killed in the war?
　　　　　　　　REV. WILLIAM SPOONER.

kills
Wild animals never kill for sport. Man is the only one to whom the torture and death of his fellow creatures is amusing in itself.
　　　　　　　　J.A. FROUDE.

kleptomaniac
A kleptomaniac is someone who helps himself because he can't help himself.
　　　　　　　　ANON.

17

MODERN QUOTATIONS

L

lamps
The lamps are going out all over Europe; we shall not see them lit again in our lifetime.
  VISCOUNT GREY OF FALLODON (*1914*).

laugh
Laugh, and the world laughs with you;
Weep, and you weep alone,
For the sad old earth must borrow its mirth,
But has trouble enough of its own.
  ELLA WHEELER WILCOX.

letting go
It's all right letting yourself go, as long as you can get yourself back.
  MICK JAGGER.

liberty
Liberty is the right to tell people what they do not want to hear.
  GEORGE ORWELL.

lie
If one cannot invent a really convincing lie, it is often better to stick to the truth.
  ANGELA THIRKELL.

---

lie A lie travels round the world while truth is putting on her boots. REV. C.H. SPURGEON. He was misquoted by James Callaghan, who said: "A lie can be halfway round the world before the truth has got its boots on.".

---

life
Life is a zoo in a jungle.
  PETER DE VRIES.

MAD DOGS AND ENGLISHMEN GO OUT IN THE MIDDAY SUN.

light
My candle burns at both ends;
It will not last the night;
But, ah, my foes, and oh my friends –
It gives a lovely light.
  EDNA ST VINCENT MILLAY.

literature
Literature is the art of writing something that will be read twice; journalism what will be grasped at once.
  CYRIL CONNOLLY.

love
Love is a many-splendoured thing.
  HAN SUYIN.

MODERN QUOTATIONS

The paths of love are rougher
Than thoroughfares of stones.
THOMAS HARDY.

Love conquers all things except poverty and toothache.
MAE WEST.

loved
'Tis better to have loved and lost
Than never to have loved at all.
ALFRED, LORD TENNYSON.

luck
We must believe in luck. For how else can we explain the success of those we don't like?
JEAN COCTEAU.

lunatic
Every reform movement has a lunatic fringe.
THEODORE ROOSEVELT.

M

mad dogs
Mad dogs and Englishmen go out in the midday sun.
NOËL COWARD.

man
Man is a clever animal who behaves like an imbecile.
ALBERT SCHWEITZER.

mankind
I love mankind; it's people I can't stand.
CHARLES M. SCHULZ.

manners
The reason nobody talks in England is because children are taught manners instead of conversation.
ROBERT MORLEY.

mathematics
Mathematics . . . possesses not only truth, but supreme beauty – a beauty cold and austere, like that of sculpture.
BERTRAND RUSSELL.

memory
Memory is more indelible than ink.
ANITA LOOS.

men
Men are like wine – some turn to vinegar, but the best improve with age.
POPE JOHN XXIII.

Some of my best leading men have been dogs and horses.
ELIZABETH TAYLOR.

mind
The human mind is like an umbrella. It functions best when open.
WALTER GROPIUS.

THE HUMAN MIND IS LIKE AN UMBRELLA. IT FUNCTIONS BEST WHEN OPEN.

MODERN QUOTATIONS

money
Money isn't everything: usually it isn't even enough.

ANON.

I don't care too much for money, Money can't buy me love.

JOHN LENNON AND PAUL MCCARTNEY.

> **money** Money is the root of all evil. THE BIBLE, *Timothy, 6:10*. actually reads: 'The love of money is the root of all evil.'.

mother
Nobody can misunderstand a boy like his own mother.

NORMAN DOUGLAS.

music
All music is singing. The ideal is to make the orchestra play like singers.

BRUNO WALTER.

I don't know anything about music. In my line you don't have to.

ELVIS PRESLEY.

I hate music, especially when it's played.

JIMMY DURANTE.

Popular music is popular because a lot of people like it.

IRVING BERLIN.

my way
I did it my way.

PAUL ANKA.

N

needs
One of the weaknesses of our age is our apparent inability to distinguish our needs from our greeds.

DON ROBINSON.

nothing
Nothing matters very much and few things matter at all.

LORD BALFOUR.

One of the lessons of history is that nothing is often a good thing to do and always a clever thing to say.

WILL DURANT.

novel
This is not a novel to be tossed aside lightly. It should be thrown with great force.

DOROTHY PARKER.

number
Well, if I called the wrong number, why did you answer the phone?

JAMES THURBER.

O

old
Anyone can get old. All you have to do is live long enough.

GROUCHO MARX.

They shall grow not old, as we that are left grow old.

LAURENCE BINYON.

Growing old is something you do if you're lucky.

GROUCHO MARX.

It's sad to grow old, but nice to ripen.

BRIGITTE BARDOT.

No man is ever old enough to know better.

HOLBROOK JACKSON.

old age
Old age is always 15 years older than I am.

BERNARD BARUCH.

I prefer old age to the alternative.

MAURICE CHEVALIER.

MODERN QUOTATIONS

opera
Nobody really sings in an opera. They just make loud noises.
AMELITA GALLI-CURCI.

optimist
The optimist proclaims that we live in the best of all possible worlds; and the pessimist fears this is true.
JAMES BRANCH CABELL.

overtakers
It's the overtakers who keep the undertakers busy.
WILLIAM PITTS.

P

pains
I can sympathize with people's pains, but not with their pleasures.
ALDOUS HUXLEY.

paradises
The true paradises are the paradises we have lost.
MARCEL PROUST.

parliament
There are three golden rules for Parliamentary speakers: 'Stand up. Speak up. Shut up.'
J.W. LOWTHER.

past
It's a waste of time thinking hard about the past. There's nothing you can do to change it.
ERTÉ (ROMAIN DE TIRTOFF).

The great thing about the past is that it's happened.
FRANK NORMAN.

The past is a foreign country: they do things differently there.
L.P. HARTLEY.

patience
Patience is not only a virtue. It pays.
B.C. FORBES.

patient
I am extraordinarily patient, provided I get my own way in the end.
MARGARET THATCHER.

pauses
The most precious things in speech are the pauses.
RALPH RICHARDSON.

people
People don't change, they only become more so.
JOHN BRIGHT-HOLMES.

The world is divided into people who do things – and people who get the credit.
DWIGHT MORROW.

Believe me, of all the people in the world, those who want the most are those who have the most.
DAVID GRAYSON.

performance
The only thing you owe to the public is a good performance.
HUMPHREY BOGART.

pessimist
A pessimist is a man who looks both ways when he's crossing a one-way street.
LAURENCE J. PETER.

Philadelphia On the whole, I'd rather be in Philadelphia. W.C. FIELDS. His actual words were "Here lies W.C. Fields. I would rather be living in Philadelphia.". He suggested that this should be engraved on his gravestone but this was not done.

MODERN QUOTATIONS

play
Play it, Sam.
> HUMPHREY BOGART (*in the film* Casablanca).

> **play** "Play it again, Sam." HUMPHREY BOGART, in the film *Casablanca*. In fact, there are two quotations, neither as printed above. The first line was spoken by Ingrid Bergman, who said: "Play it, Sam. Play *As Time Goes By*.". The second line was spoken by Humphrey Bogart, who said: "If she can stand it, I can. Play it.".

poet
A poet is, before anything else, a person who is passionately in love with language.
> W.H. AUDEN.

poetry
There's no money in poetry; but then there's no poetry in money either.
> ROBERT GRAVES.

Poetry is the supreme fiction, madame.
> WALLACE STEVENS.

politician
A politician is an animal that can sit on a fence and keep both ears to the ground.
> H.L. MENCKEN.

The only way a reporter should look at a politician is down.
> FRANK KENT.

politics
Politics is the art of the possible.
> R.A. BUTLER.

pope
Anybody can be Pope; the proof of this is that I have become one.
> POPE JOHN XXIII.

portraits
You don't change the course of history by turning the faces of portraits to the wall.
> JAWAHARLAL NEHRU.

poverty
I worked my way up from nothing to a state of extreme poverty.
> GROUCHO MARX.

Poverty is no disgrace to a man, but it is confoundedly inconvenient.
> SYDNEY SMITH.

MODERN QUOTATIONS

power
Power tends to corrupt, and absolute power corrupts absolutely.
LORD ACTON.

All power is delightful, and absolute power is absolutely delightful.
KENNETH TYNAN.

prayers
Hush! Hush! Whisper who dares! Christopher Robin is saying his prayers.
A.A.MILNE.

president
Anyone who wants to be President should have his head examined.
AVERELL HARRIMAN.

prison
It's not the people in prison who worry me. It's the people who aren't.
EARL OF ARRAN.

prisoner
A prisoner of war is a man who tries to kill you and fails, and then asks you not to kill him.
WINSTON CHURCHILL.

professor
A professor is someone who talks in someone else's sleep.
W.H. AUDEN.

progress
Progress was all right. Only it went on too long.
JAMES THURBER.

Q

qualities
It is not for our faults that we are disliked and even hated, but for our qualities.
BERNARD BERENSON.

quote
I often quote myself. It adds spice to my conversation.
GEORGE BERNARD SHAW.

R

race
It is not possible to regard our race with anything but alarm. From primeval ooze to the stars, we killed anything that stood in our way, including each other.
GORE VIDAL.

radio
Radio is a creative theatre of the mind.
WOLFMAN JACK SMITH.

rainbow
Somewhere over the rainbow,
Way up high:
There's a land that I heard of
Once in a lullaby.
E.Y. HARBURG.

MODERN QUOTATIONS

rat
The trouble with the rat race is that even if you win, you're still a rat.
LILY TOMLIN.

reality
Human kind
Cannot bear very much reality.
T.S. ELIOT.

The dignity of man lies in his ability to face reality in all its meaninglessness.
MARTIN ESSLIN.

religion
There is only one religion, though there are a hundred versions of it.
GEORGE BERNARD SHAW.

remember
Those who cannot remember the past are condemned to repeat it.
GEORGE SANTAYANA.

rich
I have been poor and I have been rich. Rich is better.
SOPHIE TUCKER.

right
Doing what's right isn't the problem. It's knowing what's right.
LYNDON B. JOHNSON.

room
All I want is a room somewhere,
Far away from the cold night air.
ALAN JAY LERNER.

rumours
I hate to spread rumours; but what else can one do with them?
AMANDA LEAR.

S

scenery
The scenery was beautiful, but the actors got in front of it.
ALEXANDER WOOLLCOTT.

school
No one who had any sense ever liked school.
LORD BOOTHBY.

Shakespeare
I know not, sir, whether Bacon wrote the words of Shakespeare, but if he did not, it seems to me he missed the opportunity of his life.
J.M. BARRIE.

ship
All I ask is a tall ship and a star to steer her by.
JOHN MASEFIELD.

show business
There's no business like show business.
IRVING BERLIN.

MODERN QUOTATIONS

Shredded Wheat
He dreamed he was eating Shredded Wheat and woke up to find the mattress half gone.
    FRED ALLEN.

sick
A youth with his first cigar makes himself sick; a youth with his first girl makes other people sick.
    MARY WILSON LITTLE.

sitting
Are you sitting comfortably? Then I'll begin.
    JULIA LANG.

sixty-four
Will you still need me, will you still feed me,
When I'm sixty-four?
    JOHN LENNON AND
    PAUL MCCARTNEY.

small
Small is beautiful.
    E.F. SCHUMACHER.

snore
Laugh and the world laughs with you; snore and you sleep alone.
    ANTHONY BURGESS.

space
Space isn't remote at all. It's only an hour's drive away if your car could go straight upwards.
    SIR FRED HOYLE.

speech
It usually takes me more than three weeks to prepare a good impromptu speech.
    MARK TWAIN.

sponge
If I believed in reincarnation, I'd come back as a sponge.
    WOODY ALLEN.

stare
What is this life, if full of care,
We have no time to stand and stare?
    W.H. DAVIES.

MODERN QUOTATIONS

stars
Two men look out through the same bars:
One sees the mud, and one the stars.
FREDERICK LANGBRIDGE.

statesman
A statesman is a politician who's been dead for ten or fifteen years.
HARRY S. TRUMAN.

When you're abroad, you're a statesman; when you're at home, you're just a politician.
HAROLD MACMILLAN.

step
That's one small step for a man, one giant leap for mankind.
NEIL A. ARMSTRONG (*The first Moon landing, 1969*)

story-teller
A good story-teller is a person who has a good memory and hopes the others haven't.
IRWIN S. COBB.

striving
Year by year we are becoming better equipped to accomplish the things we are striving for. But what are we actually striving for?
BERTRAND DE JOUVENAL.

stupidity
Stupidity is mainly just a lack of capacity to take things in.
CLIVE JAMES.

style
Style is knowing who you are, what you want to say, and not giving a damn.
GORE VIDAL.

succeed
It is not enough to succeed. Others must fail.
GORE VIDAL.

A STATESMAN IS A POLITICIAN WHO'S BEEN DEAD FOR 10 OR 15 YEARS

success
The common idea that success spoils people by making them vain, egotistic and self-complacent is erroneous – on the contrary it makes them, for the most part, humble, tolerant and kind. Failure makes people bitter and cruel.
W. SOMERSET MAUGHAM.

The toughest thing about success is that you've got to keep on being a success.
IRVING BERLIN.

survival
Survival of the fittest.
HERBERT SPENCER.

T

tact
Tact consists in knowing how to go too far.
JEAN COCTEAU.

MODERN QUOTATIONS

talent
Talent is the least important thing a performer needs, but humility is the one thing he must have.
CLARK GABLE.

taxidermist
A tall, drooping man, looking as if he had been stuffed in a hurry by an incompetent taxidermist.
P.G. WODEHOUSE.

tears
I have nothing to offer but blood, toil, tears and sweat.
WINSTON CHURCHILL (*1940*).

television
Television is an invention that permits you to be entertained in your own living-room by people you wouldn't have in your home.
DAVID FROST.

Television is for appearing on, not looking at.
NOËL COWARD.

TV is an evil medium. It should never have been invented, but since we have to live with it, let us try to do something about it.
RICHARD BURTON.

Why should people pay good money to go out and see bad films when they can stay at home and see bad television for nothing?
SAM GOLDWYN.

temptation
I can resist everything except temptation.
OSCAR WILDE.

The last temptation is the greatest treason:
To do the right deed for the wrong reason.
T.S. ELIOT.

things
It was great fun,
But it was just one of those things.
COLE PORTER.

time
Time goes, you say? Ah no!
Alas, Time stays, *we* go.
AUSTIN DOBSON.

Time present and time past
Are both perhaps present in time future
And time future contained in time past.
T.S. ELIOT.

Modern man thinks he loves something – time – when he does not do things quickly. Yet he does not know what to do with the time he gains – except kill it.
ERICH FROMM.

So little time, so little to do.
OSCAR LEVANT.

MODERN QUOTATIONS

tongue
Fighting is essentially a masculine idea; a woman's weapon is her tongue.
HERMIONE GINGOLD.

tools
Give us the tools and we'll finish the job.
WINSTON CHURCHILL.

toothpaste
Once the toothpaste is out of the tube, it's hard to get it back in.
H.R. HALDEMAN.

tragedy
It is the tragedy of the world that no-one knows what he doesn't know; and the less a man knows, the more sure he is that he knows everything.
JOYCE CARY.

train
The only way of catching a train I ever discovered is to miss the train before.
G.K. CHESTERTON.

tree
I think that I shall never see
A poem lovely as a tree.
JOYCE KILMER.

troubles
Pack up your troubles in your old kit-bag.
GEORGE ASAF.

truth
In seeking truth you have to get both sides of a story.
WALTER CRONKITE.
It has always been desirable to tell the truth, but seldom, if ever, necessary.
A.J. BALFOUR.
The first casualty when war comes is truth.
HIRAM JOHNSON.
The truth is rarely pure, and never simple.
OSCAR WILDE.
Truth is a rare and precious commodity.
We must be sparing in its use.
C.P. SCOTT.
Truth may be stranger than fiction, but fiction is truer.
FREDERIC RAPHAEL.

U

uncertainty
A little uncertainty is good for everyone.
HENRY KISSINGER.

unhappiness
Unhappiness is defined as the difference between our talents and our expectations.
EDWARD DE BONO.

unhappy
All happy families resemble one another, but each unhappy family is unhappy in its own way.
LEO TOLSTOY.

V

value
What you really value is what you miss, not what you have.
JORGE LUIS BORGES.

Venice
Venice is like eating an entire box of chocolate liqueurs at one go.
TRUMAN CAPOTE.

violence
Violence is the repartee of the illiterate.
ALAN BRIEN.

MODERN QUOTATIONS

W

walks
I like long walks, especially when they are taken by people who annoy me.
FRED ALLEN.

waltzing
And he sang as he sat and waited for his billy-boil,
'You'll come a-waltzing, Matilda, with me.'
A.B. PATERSON.

wanting
As soon as you stop wanting something, you get it.
ANDY WARHOL.

war
It is better to win the peace and to lose the war.
BOB MARLEY.
In war, you don't have to be nice, you only have to be right.
WINSTON CHURCHILL.
Mankind must put an end to war or war will put an end to mankind.
JOHN F. KENNEDY.
The quickest way of ending a war is to lose it.
GEORGE ORWELL.
War is fear cloaked in courage.
GENERAL WILLIAM WESTMORELAND.

water
You can analyse a glass of water and you're left with a lot of chemical components, but nothing you can drink.
J.B.S. HALDANE.

west
Go West, young man, Go West!
J.L.B. SOULE.

whimper
This is the way the world ends
Not with a bang but a whimper.
T.S. ELIOT.

wind
The wind of change is blowing through the continent.
HAROLD MACMILLAN.

winter
Now is the winter of our discontent made glorious summer by central heating.
JACK SHARKEY.
A cold coming we had of it,
Just the worst time of the year
For a journey, and such a long journey:
The ways deep and the weather sharp,
The very dead of winter.
T.S. ELIOT.

wisdom
Wisdom is knowing when you can't be wise
PAUL ENGLE.

women
I hate women because they always know where things are.
JAMES THURBER.
There are no ugly women, only lazy ones.
HELENA RUBINSTEIN.
Whatever women do they must do twice as well as men to be thought half as good.
CHARLOTTE WHITTON.
Women are really much nicer than men. No wonder we like them.
KINGSLEY AMIS.

wood
People love chopping wood. In this activity one immediately sees results.
ALBERT EINSTEIN.

MODERN QUOTATIONS

woodshed
Something nasty in the woodshed.
     STELLA GIBBONS.

work
I never forget that work is a curse – which is why I've never made it a habit.
     BLAISE CENDRARS.

Work expands so as to fill the time available for its completion.
     C. NORTHCOTE PARKINSON.

workers
The workers have nothing to lose but their chains. They have a world to gain. Workers of the world unite!
     KARL MARX.

world
You have to have some order in a disordered world.
     FRANK LLOYD WRIGHT.

Wren, Sir Christopher
Sir Christopher Wren
Said 'I am going to dine with some men.
If anyone calls
Say I'm designing St Paul's.'
     E.C. BENTLEY.

writer
It is by sitting down to write every morning that one becomes a writer. Those who do not do this remain amateurs.
     GERALD BRENAN.

If a writer disbelieves what he is writing, then he can hardly expect his reader to believe it.
     JORGE LUIS BORGES.

writers
Writers should be read; but neither seen nor heard.
     DAPHNE DU MAURIER.

wrong
Two wrongs don't make a right, but they make a good excuse.
     THOMAS SZASZ.

If you want to know who any of the people quoted in this book are, you can look them up in the following, alphabetically-arranged list.

Dean Acheson, politician (1893–1971)
Sir Harold Acton, man of letters (1904–)
Lord Acton (Sir J.E.E. Dalberg), historian (1834–1902)
Edward Albee, playwright (1928–)
Fred Allen, comedian (1894–1956)
Woody Allen, actor (1935–)
Muhammad Ali, boxer (1942–)
Kingsley Amis, author (1922–)
Paul Anka, singer (1941–)
Neil A. Armstrong, astronaut (1930–)
Earl of Arran, journalist (1910–1983)
George Asaf, songwriter (1880–1951)
Lady Cynthia Asquith, hostess (1887–1960)
W.H. Auden, poet (1907–1973)
A.J. Balfour, politician (1848–1930)
Brigitte Bardot, film actress (1934–)
J.M. Barrie, playwright (1860–1937)
Bernard Baruch, financier (1870–1965)
Sir Edward Beddington-Behrens, lawyer & statesman (1897–1968)
Sir Thomas Beecham, conductor (1879–1961)
Max Beerbohm, author (1872–1956)
Hilaire Belloc, author (1870–1953)
Robert Benchley, humorist (1889–1945)
Arnold Bennett, author (1867–1931)
E.C. Bentley, writer (1875–1956)
Bernard Berenson, art historian (1865–1959)
Irving Berlin, songwriter (1888–1989)
Ugo Betti, playwright (1892–1953)
Ambrose Bierce, author (1842–1914)
Josh Billings, humorist (1818–1885)
Laurence Binyon, poet (1869–1943)
Sir William Blackstone, lawyer (1723–1780)
Col. Blashford-Snell, soldier (1936–)
Humphrey Bogart, film actor (1899–1957)
Lord Boothby, politician (1900–1986)
Jorge Luis Borges, writer (1899–1986)
Gerald Brenan, writer (1894–1987)
Alan Brien, writer (1925–)
John Bright-Holmes, publisher, (current)
Rupert Brooke, poet (1887–1915)
Robert Browning, poet (1812–1889)
Luis Buñuel, film director (1900–1983)
Anthony Burgess, author (1917–)
Richard Burton, actor (1925–1984)
R.A. Butler, statesman (1902–1982)
James Branch Cabell, novelist (1879–1958)
James Callaghan, statesman (1912–)
Truman Capote, author (1924–1984)
Al Capp, cartoonist (1909–1979)
Neville Cardus, writer (1889–1975)
Dale Carnegie, writer (1888–1955)
Lewis Carroll, writer (1832–1898)
Joyce Cary, British novelist (1888–1957)
Blaise Cendrars, novelist (1887–1961)
Charlie Chaplin, film actor & producer (1889–1977)
G.K. Chesterton, author (1874–1936)
Maurice Chevalier, actor & singer (1888–1972)
Agatha Christie, author (1891–1976)
Winston Churchill, statesman (1874–1965)
Paul Claudel, composer (1868–1955)
Irwin S. Cobb, author (1876–1944)
Jean Cocteau, writer & film director (1889–1963)
Cyril Connolly, writer (1903–1974)
Gary Cooper, film actor (1901–1961)
Noël Coward, actor, composer & director (1898–1973)
Michael Crawford, actor (1942–)
Walter Cronkite, newspaper columnist (1916–)
W.H. Davies, poet (1871–1940)

Edward de Bono, lecturer in medicine (1933–)
Charles de Gaulle, statesman (1890–1970)
Peter de Vries, writer (1910–)
Austin Dobson, poet (1840–1921)
Luis Miguel Dominguin, Spanish bullfighter
Norman Douglas, author (1886–1952)
Georges Duhamel, writer (1884–1966)
Daphne du Maurier, novelist (1907–1989)
Will Durant, historian (1885–1981)
Jimmy Durante, comedian (1893–1980)
Lawrence Durrell, author (1912–1990)
Abba Eban, statesman (1915–)
Thomas A. Edison, inventor (1847–1931)
Paul Ehrlich, scientist (1932–)
Albert Einstein, mathematician (1879–1955)
T.S. Eliot, poet & author (1888–1965)
Paul Engle, poet (1908–)
Erté (Romain de Tirtoff), designer (1892–1990)
Martin Esslin, writer (1918–)
W.C. Fields, actor & comedian (1880–1946)
Robert Fitzsimmons, boxer (1862–1917)
Ian Fleming, novelist (1908–1964)
Henry Fonda, actor (1905–1982)
B.C. Forbes, publisher (1880–1954)
Anatole France, author (1844–1924)
Erich Fromm, psychologist (1900–1980)
David Frost, TV presenter (1939–)
J.A. Froude (1818–1894)
Monica Furlong, novelist (1930–)
Rose Fyleman, writer (1877–1957)
Clark Gable, film actor (1901–1961)
Amelita Galli-Curci, singer (1889–1963)
J. Paul Getty, financier (1892–1976)
Stella Gibbons, novelist (1902–1989)
Andre Gide, writer (1869–1951)
W.S. Gilbert, playwright (1836–1911)
Hermione Gingold, actress (1897–1987)
George Gissing, novelist (1857–1903)
Jean-Luc Godard, film director (1930–)
Sam Goldwyn, film producer (1882–1974)
H. Granville-Barker, actor-manager (1877–1946)
Robert Graves, poet & writer (1895–1986)
David Grayson, journalist & author (1870–1946)
Daniel S. Greenberg, science writer (1931–)
Joyce Grenfell, entertainer (1910–1980)
Viscount Grey of Fallodon, statesman (1884–1916)
Walter Gropius, architect (1883–1969)
Gene Hackman, film actor (1930–)
Lord Hailsham (Quintin Hogg), statesman (1907–)
J.B.S. Haldane, scientist (1892–1964)
H.R. Haldeman, US official (1926–)
Alex Hamilton, journalist (1917–)
Richard Hamilton, artist (1922–)
E.Y. Harburg, lyricist (1896–1981)
Sir Cedric Hardwicke, actor (1893–1964)
Thomas Hardy, novelist (1840–1928)
Averell Harriman, statesman (1891–1986)
L.P. Hartley, novelist (1895–1972)
Ian Hay, novelist (1876–1952)
Lillian Hellman, playwright (1907–1984)
W.E. Henley, poet & playwright (1849–1903)
Lord Hewart, judge (1870–1943)
Alfred Hitchcock, film director (1899–1980)
Billie Holliday, singer (1915–1959)
Bob Hope, comedian (1904–)
Lord Hore-Belisha, statesman (1893–1957)
Sir Fred Hoyle, astronomer (1915–)
Wilfred Hyde White, actor (1903–1991)
Aldous Huxley, novelist (1894–1963)

31

Holbrook Jackson, writer (1874–1978)
Mick Jagger, singer (1943–)
Clive James, TV presenter (1939–)
Randall Jarrell, critic (1914–1965)
Pope John XXIII (1881–1963)
Hiram Johnson, politician (1866–1945)
Lyndon B. Johnson, politician (1908–1973)
James Joyce, novelist (1882–1941)
Ernst Junger, writer (1895–)
Buster Keaton, comedian (1895–1966)
John F. Kennedy, statesman (1917–1963)
Frank Kent, journalist (1907–1978)
Joyce Kilmer, poet (1886–1918)
Martin Luther King, religious leader (1929–1968)
Rudyard Kipling, author (1865–1936)
Henry Kissinger, statesman (1923–)
Ronald Knox, priest & author (1888–1957)
Irving Kristol, academic (1920–)
Julia Lang, actress & broadcaster (1921–)
Frederick Langbridge, priest, poet & playwright (1849–1923)
Stephen Leacock, humorous writer (1869–1944)
Le Corbusier (Charles Edouard Jeanneret), French architect (1881–1965)
John Lennon, singer (1941–1980)
Alan Jay Lerner, playwright (1918–1986)
Oscar Levant, musician (1906–1972)
C.S. Lewis, novelist (1898–1963)
Marie Lloyd, comedienne (1870–1922)
Anita Loos, author (1893–1981)
J.W. Lowther, speaker of the House of Commons (1855–1949)
Paul McCartney, singer & composer (1942–)
Harold Macmillan, statesman (1894–1988)
Lord Mancroft, politician (1914–)
Bob Marley, singer (1945–1981)
Groucho Marx, comedian (1895–1977)
Karl Marx, political theorist (1818–1883)
John Masefield, poet & author (1878–1967)
W. Somerset Maugham, novelist (1874–1965)
Louis B. Mayer, film producer (1885–1957)
H.L. Mencken, journalist & author (1880–1956)
George Mikes, author (1912–)
Edna St Vincent Millay, American poet (1892–1950)
Jonathan Miller, doctor, writer & producer (1936–)
A.A. Milne, author (1882–1956)
Christopher Morley, playwright (1890–1957)
Robert Morley, actor (1908–1992)
Desmond Morris, author & naturalist (1928–)
Dwight Morrow, lawyer & diplomat (1873–1931)
Malcolm Muggeridge, journalist (1903–1990)
H.H. Munro – *see* 'Saki'
Jawaharlal Nehru, statesman (1889–1964)
Harold Nicolson, politician (1886–1968)
Denis Norden, writer & broadcaster (1922–)
Frank Norman, author (1930–1980)
Conor Cruise O'Brien, editor (1917–)
Laurence Olivier (Lord Olivier), actor (1907–1989)
Baroness Orczy, novelist (1865–1947)
George Orwell, novelist & essayist (1903–1950)
Lord Palmerston, statesman (1784–1865)
Dorothy Parker, writer (1893–1967)
C. Northcote Parkinson, writer (1909–)
Eric Partridge, lexicographer (1894–1979)
A.B. Paterson, writer (1864–1961)
Prince Philip (Duke of Edinburgh), (1921–)
Pablo Picasso, painter (1881–1973)
Sylvia Plath, poet (1932–1968)
Cole Porter, composer & lyricist (1891–1964)
Stephen Potter, writer (1900–1969)
Elvis Presley, singer (1935–1977)
Marcel Proust, novelist (1871–1922)
Frederic Raphael, novelist (1931–)
Nicholas Ray, film director (1911–)
Ralph Richardson, actor (1902–1983)

Ginger Rogers, film actress (1911–)
Franklin D. Roosevelt, statesman (1882–1945)
Theodore Roosevelt, statesman (1858–1919)
Leo C. Rosten, writer (1908–)
A.L. Rowse, academic (1903–)
Helena Rubinstein, beautician (1872–1965)
John Ruskin, poet & critic (1819–1900)
Bertrand Russell, philosopher (1872–1970)
'Saki' (H.H. Munro), novelist (1870–1916)
Lord Samuel, statesman (1870–1963)
George Santayana, philosopher (1863–1952)
Charles M. Schulz, cartoonist (1922–)
E.F. Schumacher, economist (1911–1977)
Albert Schweitzer, doctor & missionary (1875–1965)
C.P. Scott, journalist (1846–1932)
George C. Scott, film actor (1926–)
Pete Seeger, singer (1919–)
H. Gordon Selfridge, store owner (1864–1947)
Robert Service, poet (1874–1958)
Dr Theodor Seuss, writer (1904–)
Bill Shankly, soccer manager (1918–1981)
George Bernard Shaw, playwright (1856–1950)
B.F. Skinner, American psychiatrist (1904–)
Stevie Smith, poet (1902–1971)
Sydney Smith, clergyman & essayist (1771–1845)
Willie 'The Lion' Smith, jazz musician (1895–1973)
Wolfman Jack Smith, disc jockey
J.L.B. Soule, editor & author (1815–1891)
Herbert Spencer, philosopher (1820–1903)
Laurence Stallings, writer (1894–1968)
Lincoln Steffens, journalist (1866–1936)
John Steinbeck, novelist (1902–1968)
Wallace Stevens, poet (1879–1955)
Han Suyin, novelist (1917–)
Thomas Szasz, psychiatrist (1920–)
Elizabeth Taylor, film actress (1932–)
Lord Taylor of Gryfe, businessman (1912–)
Alfred, Lord Tennyson, poet (1809–1892)
Margaret Thatcher, stateswoman (1925–)
Angela Thirkell, author (1890–1961)
Dylan Thomas, poet (1914–1953)
James Thurber, humorist & cartoonist (1894–1961)
Leo Tolstoy, novelist (1828–1910)
Lily Tomlin, comedienne (1939–)
Harry S. Truman, statesman (1884–1972)
Sophie Tucker, entertainer (1884–1966)
Mark Twain, novelist (1835–1910)
Kenneth Tynan, critic (1927–1980)
Peter Ustinov, actor, author & playwright (1921–)
H.W. Van Loon, author (1882–1944)
Queen Victoria (1819–1901)
Gore Vidal, author (1925–)
Edgar Wallace, novelist (1875–1932)
Henry Wallace, politician (1888–1965)
Bruno Walter, musician (1876–1962)
Andy Warhol, artist & film-maker (1926–1988)
Orson Welles, actor & director (1915–1985)
H.G. Wells, novelist (1886–1946)
Mae West, film actress (1893–1980)
Gen. William Westmoreland, soldier (1914–)
James McNeill Whistler, artist (1834–1903)
Charlotte Whitton, writer (1896–1975)
Ella Wheeler Wilcox, poet (1850–1919)
Oscar Wilde, playwright (1854–1900)
Harry Williams, songwriter (1874–1924)
P.G. Wodehouse, novelist & lyricist (1881–1975)
Tom Wolfe, writer (1931–)
Virginia Woolf, novelist (1882–1941)
Alexander Woollcott, critic (1887–1943)
Frank Lloyd Wright, architect (1869–1959)
W.F. Yeames, painter (1835–1918)
W.B. Yeats, poet (1865–1939)
Israel Zangwill, playwright & novelist (1864–1926)
Adolph Zukor, film producer (1873–1976)